REVERSE ENGINEER
YOUR FUTURE

STOP WAITING FOR SUCCESS
GO OUT AND MAKE IT HAPPEN NOW

REVERSE ENGINEER YOUR FUTURE

PAUL JAMES

LIONCREST
PUBLISHING

REVERSE ENGINEER YOUR FUTURE

Stop Waiting for Success—Go Out and Make It Happen Now

ISBN   978-1-61961-754-4 *Paperback*

976-1-61961-755-1 *Ebook*

CONTENTS

—

INTRODUCTION

I could barely see through the windshield, the snow was falling so hard. The freeway was slick. I was in West Bend, Wisconsin, driving back from a day of classes at nursing school in Milwaukee. As I drove across an overpass, I lost control of the car. There's never enough salt for the winter roads where I live, and I must have hit black ice. The steering wheel started spinning out of control—first left, then right; I couldn't get the car straightened out no matter how hard I tried. My life flashed before my eyes as the vehicle spun in circles and then flew off the overpass.

I was experiencing bad car karma; it was my second accident in two years. About a year and a half earlier, I was driving to the mall with Kari, then my girlfriend and now my wife. We were on Calhoun Road in Brookfield, outside Milwaukee. It was around five o'clock on a nice summer day, and we were just going to hang out for a while after work. My car was a junky blue Pontiac I'd bought for $800 from a guy I worked with. I had recently sold my truck to pay for nursing school. That black Chevy Silverado had been my baby—I'd bought it brand new when I turned sixteen with money I'd earned myself. But I felt selling it was worth the sacrifice because it meant being able to go to nursing school. Even though the Pontiac looked low rent, I was proud of it because I owned it outright and it worked great.

Kari and I were at a stoplight when I looked in the rear-view mirror and saw a white truck barreling toward us. I was frozen for a second, but then I realized I had to do something, or it would crash into us. I quickly tried to pull off the road, but the truck's driver tried to do the same, and he rear-ended us. We went flying, and my car was totaled. The airbags deployed, and while I emerged without a scratch, Kari got whiplash that affects her to this day. Plus, the accident aggravated a knee condition she'd had since she was a kid. We never found out exactly why the driver of the white truck hit us; as far as we know, he wasn't drunk but more likely distracted.

At that time, I was already stretched financially because

of school. I had to take out a $3,000 loan to buy another car—an old gold Nissan Maxima. It ended up having one problem after another—from worn tires to a leaky water pump—that required a constant influx of cash. The Nissan was the car I was in when I hit black ice and flew off the overpass in the middle of that crazy Wisconsin snowstorm.

Returning to that night: by the grace of God or whatever you want to call it, I landed in a ditch facing oncoming traffic. I was shaken up, but I was OK. I wasn't sure what to do, so I just sat there for a while, the snow falling all around me. It was so quiet. Eventually, I called my mom and asked her whether she thought I should call the police. She recommended it, so I did.

I waited for what seemed like an eternity, but the police never came. Finally, I decided to try to get out of the ditch myself. I revved up the engine and pulled the car up and out to the shoulder. I managed to find a gap between cars on the freeway, crossed over to the other side, and turned for home. I was exhausted from the shock of what had just happened, but I was safe.

As I drove home, I started thinking about the discouraging circumstances of the past couple of years. It wasn't just that first car crash or that there never seemed to be enough money, even though I was working full time at Walmart while going to school. It was that Kari and I had just gotten married and wanted to start our lives in our own place, but we didn't have enough money to do it. We were living at my brother's house in his garage-turned-clubhouse. There was no bathroom and not enough quiet. In addition, I had invested so much financially and emotionally into nursing school, but I was now having serious doubts about whether it was the right path for me.

It's hard to predict when or where defining moments are going to happen for us, but as I drove, I had one of those moments. Even though I hadn't been hurt when my car skidded into the ditch, the experience felt like the final straw in a series of unfortunate events. Instead of feeling unglued, I began to feel a strength inside of me that I hadn't felt before. Despite everything that had happened or was happening, I knew I was going to get out of the hole I was in. I was going to climb out the same way I had just driven out of that ditch.

I didn't know how, but I knew I could, and I would.

I felt determined that I wasn't going to be average, and I wasn't going to let life make me average. I was going to use everything that had happened in the past to make me better, not worse. To an outsider, that period of my life could have looked like a downward spiral. But that night, slowly driving home in the snow, I knew that wasn't the case and that I was going to be the master of my destiny.

I knew something big was going to happen, and it did. As a result, today I'm a successful Internet marketer.

KNOW YOU ARE DESTINED FOR MORE

If you're feeling uncertain or uneasy about where you are in life, I wrote this book for you. I want you to know that the past and the present don't have to shape the future. Most people have an instinct—like I did—that something big and amazing is going to happen to turn things around for them. Whether you're about to graduate from college and are looking for a great job, or you're a struggling actor trying to land a pivotal role, life has more in store for you than you can imagine.

The magic of being able to drastically change your life the way I did is an equal-opportunity experience. I'm no different from you. In fact, I consider myself pretty average: I didn't grow up with any special privileges. I wasn't born with any superpowers. Yet as an Internet marketer, I've been able to create a life that is fulfilling beyond my wildest dreams, personally and professionally. I feel like I found the golden ticket like Charlie in *Charlie and the Chocolate Factory*. I want you to find it, too, and

I'm going to show you how, especially when it comes to using challenges to propel you forward. Many times, we let problems encapsulate us, and then we feel trapped inside a problem bubble. But what if problems are just a sign you're growing and on your road to success? What if problems make you a better person?

My promise is to do everything possible to inspire and motivate you by sharing the key insights that have shaped my thinking and success. We all look at life through our own filters shaped by different things, although mainly by our families and past experiences. Some of those filters are clear and give us razor-sharp vision, but some are dark and cloudy, and they create an inaccurate view. The bottom line is that our filters affect our mindsets, and our mindsets affect how we respond to whatever is happening.

If you've been struggling and feel depressed or cynical about the future, my goal is that after you finish this book, you'll think differently about life—you'll start thinking that life is working in your favor. The most successful people think this way, and they're always adapting to unforeseen events and challenges from that mindset.

WORK WITH THE CURRENT

I go kayaking as much as I can on the Milwaukee River

near my house. The starting point is a dam, and when I first load in and head downstream, I always see tons of wildlife, especially turtles making their way in and out of the water on the banks. Then the scenery changes, and I'm kayaking through downtown West Bend, past all the shops and businesses and people going through their day. The scenery changes again pretty quickly, and I'm kayaking through the woods and the silence.

The whole trip can be awesome because you have the chance to see a little bit of everything. But it's only a good trip if you're going *with* the current. If you try to go against the current, it's hard work, and you eventually tire out before the end of the route. You miss the scenery. When you're going with the current, you can enjoy it all. That's what I want to teach you in this book: how to go with the current and position life to work for you, not against you.

1

MY STORY

I **WAS AROUND TWELVE YEARS OLD WHEN I**
first saw the magic trick. My dad had taken me to
a magic store called Theophilus on the south side
of Milwaukee. Today, Theophilus is no longer in
business, but when it was, it was one of the most popu-
lar magic stores in the country. It was owned by a former
professional magician named Fred Jurgensen who loved
his field and selling people famous tricks like The Guil-
lotine. The store also had everything a kid could want,
including fake vomit.

The trick I saw when I was twelve is called Stratosphere.
The magician puts three balls in a tube; the balls are different colors, like red, green, and yellow. Then he or she
covers up the tube. When the tube is uncovered—voilà!
The balls have changed places. What's really happening
is that there's an extra ball inside the tube that the audi-

ence can't see, and when you load the first three balls, the invisible fourth pushes one of them down.

I was blown away the first time I saw Stratosphere, and I knew I had to buy and learn the trick for myself. That was the beginning of my fascination with magic. I got hooked on watching magic shows, and by the time I was around thirteen, I had my own business cards (*Paul James, Master Magician*) and was booking gigs like birthday and Christmas parties. But I was already thinking ahead and anticipating a defining moment, like being discovered in Vegas and becoming the next David Copperfield.

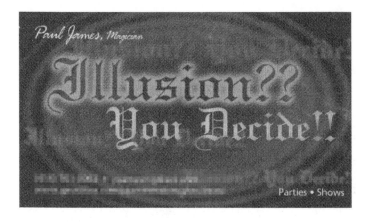

This mindset—call it big breakism—stayed with me as I got older. When I joined a band, it was about getting a record deal and becoming famous. When I started my Internet marketing business, I thought that by connecting with a celebrity in my field, doors would open, my message would get out to the world, and millions of dollars would follow.

I'm not sure how I starting believing that life is all about getting a big break, but as I said in the introduction, our lives are usually colored by our parents and our experiences. Growing up, my mom, like many other people, was a big believer in the power of luck. She read her horoscope nearly every morning. When my birthday rolled around, she'd read me mine so I would know what the year was going to bring. She bought Powerball lottery tickets at the BP gas station near our house every week and was always finding lucky pennies on the street. She believed luck was a force out there in the world and that it could rain down on you out of nowhere and change your life. Her mindset rubbed off on me.

As I built a successful online business, over time I realized I had it wrong. There wasn't going to be a single moment or person who would transform my life. I learned this after I tried to make those moments happen, and they didn't. I learned this after connecting and making business plans with superstars in my industry who didn't follow through. Eventually, I stopped looking for my big break and decided to focus on being an entrepreneur who made his own luck.

I shifted from a fantasy mindset about life to a *realistic* one. For example, I'm in the process of learning how to rock climb. Before I started, I had an idea in my head of how cool it would be to rock climb. But once you're actually climbing, fear sets in. You have to make real adjustments and figure out what you're going to do so that you don't fall.

Right now, I'm learning how to lead climb. The leader goes up a wall or a cliff and clips the rope to anchor points on the ascent. Doing so makes a way for other climbers. The leader wears a harness with a rope connected to the belayer, a person on the ground who lets out the rope a little bit at a time as the climber ascends. Even though you have the second system to ensure that the belayer can arrest a fall, there's a difference between thinking you are mentally prepared for a fall and whether you stay calm when it happens.

The other day, I was about twenty-five feet in the air, lead climbing at an indoor climbing gym near my house. I reached for an anchor point, slipped, and fell fifteen feet. It was terrifying. My heart raced, and I blacked out for a second. Now I really know what it's like to fall and about the critical need for a backup system to catch me.

The point is that people say there's no substitute for experience, and they're right. The experience of creating and running a successful business changed how I thought and what I wanted to do. Instead of making my goal to become famous, I realized that my ultimate passion is helping people to build profitable businesses and achieve the lifestyles they want through turning their ideas into products or services.

Whether your goal is creating a business or making a significant change in your personal life, the steps I'm going to share are the same. I'm going to offer my guidance and expertise to help you connect the dots and get from an idea to an ultimate goal.

HOW YOU THINK MATTERS

With the right mindset, you can achieve anything. I'm going to show you how I developed a new mindset through various examples from my career and my personal life. While working for a heating, ventilation, and air conditioning company, for example, I discovered how you can almost always figure anything out, no matter how complicated a task or a problem seems at first. From being in a band, I discovered how to create a tribe and inspire and motivate them. While I was in nursing school, I learned the power of knowing when you're on the right road for yourself or the wrong one. From starting my own Internet marketing business, I learned about the importance of following your unique vision.

In addition, having personal struggles—going against the wishes of family when it came to getting married and changing my career direction—influenced and motivated my path.

My personal and professional experiences led to the development of a new mindset centered on the following concepts:

- **Reframe your struggles.** Even if you don't understand why certain events have happened, looking at them in a different way can help you.
- **Define who you want to be.** This can be a trial-and-error process as you learn how to get specific.
- **Leverage past experiences.** Whether they're things that happened with your family, career, or even the skills you picked up from hobbies, pieces of gold exist that you can mine to forward your momentum today.
- **Be prepared to steer or change course.** Learning to identify when you're off-course is a key skill.
- **It's not all in the timing.** Instead of waiting for a breakthrough moment, focus on using your time well. It's always the right time.
- **Small wins add up.** Getting started is the hardest part

of reaching any goal. Try giving yourself a smaller goal to hit in the beginning, one that's almost impossible not to reach. You'll feel great accomplishing it and then begin leveraging small successes into big ones.

Using these concepts changed my life, and I want you to use them to change yours. They're my version of a GPS. I also want to emphasize that the more focused and disciplined you are, the better your outcome.

ENTERING THE WORLD OF WORK

I started working for a heating company when I was fifteen. I was the kind of kid for whom school was fairly tortuous. It's not that I wasn't smart—I just learned best by doing, not by sitting in a classroom chained to a desk. Sitting at a desk wasn't purposeful for me. By the time I started working at the heating company, I was on the verge of getting kicked out of school, in part from skipping so many classes. I would cut and go home and play *Grand Theft Auto* and other video games.

I started out doing grunt work at the heating company, like cutting the grass around the office building. This took me an hour and a half with a push mower, and then I'd spend another couple of hours trimming the hedges. It would get extremely hot in the summer, but I didn't care. I loved accomplishing tasks, even if they seemed menial to other people. When I was done with the grass and the bushes, I would hang out and observe what was going on at the company.

Eventually, I started getting sent out into the field when other workers didn't show up or when employees needed help carrying an especially heavy air conditioner or heating unit. I quickly became a sponge; I wanted to absorb and learn everything about the company and what its employees did. I loved the environment. The world of work felt like home to me.

Every aspect of the business intrigued me, even things like making sheet metal. You've got to make sheet metal when you're taking out an old furnace and the new one is a different size. The new one is usually shorter. You need to build a component that will line up the new furnace with the old ductwork. Some days, after I'd finished cutting the grass, I'd go to the back of the shop and watch people make sheet metal. They used giant shears to cut it to the right dimensions. This wasn't boring to me because I was learning how to do something new. Also, a big part of my personality is being a problem solver, and I liked the fact that we were solving the problem of how to get a new unit to work in an old space. It was like being back at Theophilus trying to figure out the anatomy of a magic trick.

I learned every aspect of installation, from putting in gas lines and thermostats to figuring out where and how to vent the exhaust. Over time, I became the lead installer. I worked my way up and ended up managing the office. I was doing accounts payable and receivable, dispatching and scheduling, and hiring and firing.

I envisioned staying at the company forever. But then, business began to fall off for various reasons—unpaid work from city contracts and seasonal slowdowns among them. I got assigned grunt work again, along with service and installations. I had liked being a manager, and my passion for being in the field wasn't there anymore. That's when I realized the company wasn't my destiny. I knew I needed to find a different path.

BEING IN A BAND, BEING A CREATOR

While I was working at the heating company, I joined my first band, Single Serving Friends. I was nineteen, and I answered the band's ad looking for a guitar player on a website called *Milwaukee Rocks*. I downloaded their music—pop/rock—and learned a few of their songs so I could audition for them. When I got to the audition, they needed a keyboard player, too. I had actually taught myself the keyboard parts as well, and so I got the job.

I had gotten into guitar when I was seven or eight years old, when my friend Bobby's dad bought him one. Bobby ended up getting more into drums, but I learned how to play his guitar. We would jam together every other weekend in my basement, pretending to be a band and playing stuff like Metallica. We were mini-metalheads.

As we grew up, Bobby eventually moved on to other things, but I got serious about music. Part of the reason was that I loved to perform. It's strange because I'm generally an introvert, but when I was onstage, I loved expressing a different part of my identity. I'm also a creator—meaning I love to make things—and putting together a performance was about creating something out of nothing. That all lends itself to what I do today, which is create products and information for people, as well as teach them.

I eventually left Single Serving Friends and started my own pop/rock band, Lights, Camera, Action. It originally began as a solo project and evolved into a full-fledged band. I loved the freedom of heading up my own venture, and it forced me to figure out how to write songs instead of playing other people's.

The music industry was experiencing some of its first tremors of change. MySpace, not Facebook, was a force back then, and I started trying to figure out how to get social media followers. Fairly quickly, Lights, Camera, Action grew a large audience of nearly forty thousand fans who listened to our music online.

One of the reasons our fan base grew so quickly was that I was treating the band like a business. I had learned a little bit about marketing from the heating company, so for me, the purpose of the band wasn't just to play music but to also make money. I created merchandise, like T-shirts, for us to sell at shows. I made a schedule of how many shows we needed to book per month to reach financial milestones. I insisted we practice regularly to keep our edge musically. The rest of the band members weren't as serious as I was, but I wanted more than just getting together to jam.

I had dreams of getting us a record deal. I thought the attention of a major label would change my life. I did everything possible to make it happen. It didn't. But it became one more step toward ultimately discovering my calling and helping people find theirs. I'll talk more about this later in the book.

NURSING SCHOOL

One day, I was out in the field for the heating company. I was sitting in the company truck for a few minutes with a childhood friend, Wally. I had gotten him a job at the company, and he was working as my helper that day on an installation. We started talking about how cool it would be to get into the health field. We were both passionate about science and had aced chemistry and biology in high school. As a problem solver, I loved the detective work it took to figure out what was wrong with people when they were sick.

We began to talk more about going to nursing school and whether it was a good idea. At the time, there was a nursing shortage in my state and across the country, and salaries were roughly $60,000 to $70,000 a year. I had the pressure of bills to pay, and I was looking for work that helped people and meant something to me. I was close to twenty years old, and I was trying to be as responsible as possible. As Wally and I discussed nursing school more, it all came together. I said to him, "Why am I sitting here debating it? I'm just going to do it."

When I got into nursing school, my parents were over-the-top excited. I would be the first person in my family to go to college. My family's approval meant the world to me. I decided to get a nursing degree for starters and work in the field for a number of years. Later, I might continue my schooling and become a doctor or a nurse practitioner. In the beginning, I felt a sense of peace and possibility around the decision, even though I was paying my own way. Little did I know how much debt was going to pile up.

A DOUBLE-EDGED SWORD

Although going to nursing school had the positive mojo of both feeling like the right decision and pleasing my family, all was not well at home and work. What I came to understand is that you can't separate your personal problems from your professional ones. They inform and influence each other. They add to your stress, but they also motivate you to move forward.

After I left the heating company to go to nursing school and sold my truck to help finance it, Kari and I both started working at Walmart to pay for gas and other expenses. We also began to share the vision of our future with her parents, which included getting engaged soon. That didn't go over well, as they had a different plan in mind—one that involved Kari staying at home and going to college.

Kari's dad was understandably worried about his daughter and how we would make it on our own at such a young age while working Walmart. Even though we weren't in the Internet marketing business at the time, we still knew we would do whatever it took to make our marriage—and our lives—work.

In Walmart uniform, before work.

Something shifted inside me after Kari's father expressed his doubt. I knew I had to prove to him that we would make it. Maybe it was primal; I don't know. But his fears were rocket fuel when it came to propelling me to figure out how to create an amazing future.

Meanwhile, my living situation was about to take a turn for the worse. It was the middle of the country's mortgage crisis, and my mom's adjustable-rate mortgage began climbing. She, like so many other people, ended up losing her house.

My brother was generous enough to let my mom, me, and Kari move in with him. He had a big house in West Bend on a couple of acres. It had two garages. One garage was remodeled into a small apartment; that's where my mom settled in. It had everything: a bedroom, living room, and kitchen, plus a washer and dryer. The other garage was dubbed the clubhouse. It was a twelve-by-twenty-foot room with a pool table and TV where my brother and his family and friends would hang out. No bathroom.

Kari and I, our black cat, Ling-Ling, and our Yorkie, Tinkerbell, moved into the clubhouse. Whenever we had to use the bathroom, shower, or do laundry, we had to go up to the big house. We were grateful to my brother for giving us a place to live, but walking through the snow to go to the bathroom during the Wisconsin winter wasn't fun. The surroundings were often noisy, even in the middle of the night, and it was hard to get enough sleep. In hindsight, it wasn't an ideal situation, but we were determined to make it work.

2

REFRAME YOUR STRUGGLES

—

MOST EVERYONE, ESPECIALLY PARents with sick kids, believe that a fever is a bad thing, but when I was in nursing school, I learned that's not always the case. A low-grade fever is often a sign, for example, that the body is killing harmful microbes. A fever jump-starts the immune system to fight infection. In many situations, doctors and nurses know that a fever is a sign that a person's body is going through a temporary challenge and will come out the other side.

When I was in nursing school, I was struggling, but I didn't know that it was just a symptom, like a fever, that something deeper was going on. I was driving nearly an hour to classes every day and moving my car roughly every forty-five minutes so I wouldn't get a parking ticket. I was working at Walmart and studying like crazy. Money was tight; even coming up with gas money was a challenge. Once I got home at night, the environment at the clubhouse was chaotic and, as mentioned, I never got enough sleep. I was living day to day, trying to make it all work. After a while, I felt numb, like the zombies trudging through the video game *Call of Duty*.

THE COMMON DENOMINATOR

The one thing every struggle has in common is you. The first time I started to realize this was when I was in the studio one day recording with Lights, Camera, Action. As our producer mixed a track, one of our band members complained to him nonstop for a half hour about his girlfriend and about how national and local politics were affecting him personally. Finally, our producer said, "You can't fix what's going on around you. You have to realize that you're the root of all your problems."

A light bulb went off for me.

I began to learn that even though many elements around you are out of your control, there are things you can do to shift any given situation. For example, one of my present-day Internet marketing clients was working crazy hours at a bank and didn't have any time to spend with his family. Even though he was exhausted most of the time, he kept looking for a solution and eventually found my work. Nine months after I taught him search engine optimization (SEO), he was able to quit his job. Now he runs an SEO business with his son.

What I'm talking about here is *shifting* a situation, not fighting it. In the martial art of aikido, you're always taught to go with the momentum of your opponent. By doing so, your opponent's own force often takes them off balance, and they tumble off the mat. In the same way, when you shift how you're viewing a challenging situation in your life instead of battling it, things change.

Learning how to shift life started for me in a small way. When I'd get home at night after nursing school and work, instead of binge-watching *House* on Netflix or playing guitar, I'd get online for an hour and research additional ways to make extra money. I became disciplined. I became a learner. Most of all, I eventually became someone who took matters into his own hands rather than trusting another person or an institution to guide me.

I was learning that even though life can feel out of control, there's always something you can do differently to move your situation forward. You don't have to know the master plan. You just have to start feeling a level of power from inside yourself. That happens when you get outside your comfort zone. For many people, this realization happens when they hit rock bottom. I wasn't at rock bottom, but I was adrift and trying like crazy to swim to shore.

OUTSIDE YOUR COMFORT ZONE

One of the key ways to get outside your comfort zone is to trust your gut. My journey to becoming a successful entrepreneur started when I stopped looking for external approval. For me, that grew out of realizing how short life is. We're on this spinning blue-green marble for a heartbeat, and we've got to make the most of it.

Up until I started to become dissatisfied with nursing school, I'd always done what I thought other people wanted from me, instead of asking myself what I wanted. I'm not certain why; maybe it's because I'm the youngest in my family. Research shows that youngest kids often grow up to be followers because we're used to older siblings bossing us around. Growing up, I'd always fallen in line and didn't think too much of it. But as I became more disciplined and committed to self-growth, I began to think for myself. It was scary and exciting at the same time.

Struggle can become a comfort zone in itself. Despite how uncomfortable I was living with my brother, I was still surrounded by family. Even though I was questioning nursing school, it was still a culturally approved and predictable track. I realized that in order to get out of my comfort zone, I needed to take actions to challenge myself. If I didn't, I'd be like a caterpillar that turned to mush because it never struggled to get out of the cocoon and become a butterfly.

Everyone makes fun of helicopter parents these days. Mine weren't that way, but the whole phenomenon points to the fact that in our culture, we don't have solid rituals for people in their late teens and twenties that mark the transition to becoming an adult. In Kenya, boys in the Maasai tribe leave their families and live in a warrior camp, creating a line between boyhood and manhood. In the United States, we don't do anything like that. I didn't realize it at the time, but when I started to challenge myself, I was crossing over into a new phase of my life.

I don't think we go outside our comfort zones unless something forces us to do so. When I was working for the heating company, I fell twenty feet off a ladder once when we were replacing a chimney liner. That, in part, was why I realized I needed to find a new path. When I was a nursing student, cleaning up poop after a patient made me realize I couldn't do that for the long haul. I had to start listening to my intuition to find a new way both times. Moving outside your comfort zone is simple, but in the beginning stages, it's not necessarily easy.

When I was growing up, my family was constantly moving around. From the ages of six to fourteen, I was always the new kid. It was a struggle, but it forced me to learn how to make connections and talk to people. The benefit of constantly being forced outside my comfort zone growing up became apparent to me when I went to college. Unlike other freshman, I was used to being thrown into an unfamiliar environment where I had to make friends. Then, when I started my business, my new-kid training really kicked in. I had no problem making phone calls to strangers, building business contacts, and constantly encountering unfamiliar circumstances.

However, going outside our comfort zones means we'll almost always immediately face the disapproval of others. That's what happened when I left nursing school. My family had been so proud that I was the first to go to college. When I quit, most of them were disappointed, doubtful that I'd done the right thing, and didn't think I'd find another career as meaningful and well paying. They wanted the best for me, and they wanted me to finish what I'd started.

But entrepreneurs are wired differently from other people. Lori Greiner, the venture capitalist from *Shark Tank*, has a saying: "Entrepreneurs work eighty hours a week so they don't have to work forty hours a week." Grenier got a communications degree from Loyola University Chicago but chucked it after graduation to find her own way. Now she's a well-adjusted, happy millionaire and the queen of QVC. She knew a traditional path wasn't for her, and as much as I hated letting my family down, so did I.

THE VALUE OF DISAPPOINTING PEOPLE

Reframing your personal struggles is important as well. As I mentioned in chapter one, when Kari and I moved in together, her parents were disappointed with her decision to do so, despite the fact that we had been dating for years. Kari's family is extremely religious, and they did not want us to live in sin. However, we were simply not in a position to finance a wedding at that time. We needed to wait to get married in order to have the kind of wedding that we had envisioned.

Kari and I had met out on the music scene and had clicked. We had the same values and morals: we liked hanging out in clubs to see local bands but weren't into partying. We're also similar in that we prefer not to judge people. On our first date, I went over to Kari's house and her pet duck, Waffles, tried to bite me. Thankfully, Kari didn't take it as a bad omen.

As I was redefining myself, we were doing the same thing

as a couple. We were going against other people's expectations. They were well-intentioned expectations; they simply weren't ours. As I mentioned earlier, Kari's parents wanted her to go to college. When they found out about our moving in together, they wanted her to immediately move back home. Neither was going to happen. It was a tense time.

When Kari's parents realized she wasn't coming home, they offered to finance our wedding. We were initially grateful, but their expectations soon became overwhelming. Plans started to get out of control. More conflict erupted, and we knew that we couldn't move forward with having them pay for the wedding.

Today, we both have a good relationship with Kari's parents. We respect and love one another. But at the time, the theme that kept emerging was that as a couple, Kari and I felt as if we were living to please other people. Everyone knows that feeling, and it's not a good one. Back then, we realized that no matter how hard it was, we were going to have to do what was right for us.

Every parent has a vision for his or her child, and Kari's folks were following theirs. We ultimately got married on our own terms, and the struggle and pain we went through motivated us to succeed personally and professionally.

TAKING RESPONSIBILITY

As I said at the beginning of this chapter, one of the most powerful things you can do in your life is to stop looking at your struggles as problems. Use them instead to provide more motivation in your pursuit of becoming a successful entrepreneur.

One of the misconceptions people have is that finding their way is a straight line. It's more like a constant zigzag. My employment struggle at the heating company motivated me to go to nursing school. Realizing nursing school wasn't for me inspired me to become more disciplined and pursue becoming an entrepreneur. Meanwhile, our struggles to please Kari's parents drove both of us even further to excel. So did our desire to change our living situation.

The key is taking responsibility. Nobody can change your life but you. It was scary to eventually leave my brother's house for an apartment, but I knew I had to put myself in a situation where there was no one else to ask for help or to fall back on.

When you trust yourself, stop listening to naysayers, and give up looking for external approval and validation, you can succeed even if the deck is stacked against you.

What I also did during this time was learn how to "reverse engineer" where I wanted to go. I'll go into more detail about this in the following chapters. But in short, I began to analyze how successful people became that way. I learned what made them tick, how they thought, and how they ran their companies. I picked them apart and used what I learned to help me grow as a person and an entrepreneur. By doing this, I changed my life. So can you.

3

DEFINE WHO YOU WANT TO BE

—

THE BIGGEST MISTAKE PEOPLE MAKE WHEN they focus on their careers is setting goals that are too generic, such as "to make a bunch of money." Instead, you have to ask yourself detailed questions such as the following: Exactly how much do I want to make? What am I going to do with that money? What kind of house do I want to live in? What kind of car do I want to drive?

When you clearly define your goals, you can see if you're on the path toward hitting them. If you're struggling and things aren't going your way, it's time to get real and question whether you're on the right track.

When I was in Lights, Camera, Action, my goal was to become a famous musician. I looked at Pete Wentz of the rock band Fall Out Boy and thought about how cool it would be to have a fan base and a clothing line like his. The band's drummer, Andy Hurley, is from my hometown in Wisconsin, so the dream didn't seem far-fetched.

I made one effort after another to catch fame but kept hitting dead ends. I got in touch with singer/songwriter/ dancer Jason Derulo's entertainment attorney. He was extremely interested in our band at one point, but nothing panned out. I talked to managers at top recording companies, including Hollywood Records, Disney's label. At Hollywood Records, I was offered a songwriting opportunity, but that fizzled as well.

I finally gave up. By doing so, I realized that when I was admiring and dreaming of being in the position of bands like Fall Out Boy, with their audiences full of screaming fans, I was looking at an end result. I wasn't looking at how they got there. I wasn't thinking about the ten years leading up to those concerts and the work that had been put in day after day.

As I thought more about what it would be like to be a famous musician, I realized that the lifestyle didn't suit me or Kari. We didn't want to be on the road touring most of the year and living out of a van. We didn't want to spend years scrambling to buy groceries or pay bills, which is what most musicians end up doing. As I began thinking specifically about what I didn't want, what I did want started to become clearer.

BELIEVE IT FIRST

If you're struggling like I was, it's time to take a more holistic approach to your business and personal life. Ask yourself, "Where do I really want to be?"

I learned this approach in part from Robert Kiyosaki, the American businessman, investor, and author of *Rich Dad Poor Dad*. The book details his journey to financial success by analyzing the differences between, and advice from, his two dads: his real father and the father of his best friend. *Rich Dad Poor Dad* stresses visualization.

Kari and I starting driving around fancy subdivisions looking at properties. Even though we didn't have the money to buy anything, we shopped as if we did. We grabbed the real estate pamphlets from the box on For Sale signs and pored over them. We decided we wanted a big place in a good neighborhood with an open floor plan. We wanted land to zoom across in ATVs and for privacy.

The next thing I did was go out and look at cars. I test-drove a bunch before I settled on a black Mercedes-Benz SUV.

I want you to do the same thing: go shopping for some of your biggest dreams. As a result of acting "as if," I started to believe that I'd be able to have these things. I didn't know how just yet, but I started to trust that I'd find a way.

Meanwhile, around this time, I had started working in affiliate marketing and was dabbling in SEO. I was beginning to make money—not a lot but enough to signify potential.

I tallied up what I'd need to earn each year in order to afford our dream house, the Mercedes, and other aspects of the kind of life I wanted to live. I worked out how much I needed to earn a year, a month, a week, and even a day to meet those goals. It came out to a six-figure income.

DREAM LIFE CALCULATION	MONTHLY COST
5,000 Sq Ft House	$3,000
Property Taxes	$300
Mercedes-Benz	$1,000
Gas & Electric Utilities	$300
Cell Phone	$160
Internet/Cable	$160
Food	$1,200
Gas For Car	$600
Boat	$300
Spending Money	$1,000
Total Monthly Cost	**$8,020**

My next step was to figure out what I needed to charge

for my products and services in order to sell enough to hit my salary targets. I quantified it into specifics, such as needing five new clients and selling five products a day. I calculated how much money I needed to make tomorrow versus how much I'd need to earn five years out.

I want you to do the same thing. Figure out how much you need to make and break it down into specifics, whether that's clients, products, or an hourly rate. Say you're a website designer. If you make $1,000 for each website you design, and want to make $5,000 a month, then you'll need to sell five a month. If you sell subscriptions for delivering high-end beef jerky each month to offices, calculate about how many accounts you'll need to reach your dream salary.

CALCULATING THE TRADE-OFF

When you've specified your dreams and calculated what you need to earn to make them happen, the next step is to figure out if the trade-offs are worth it. If you calculate that you need to work one hundred hours a week to afford a certain house or car, you'll have a better sense of whether you're willing to go that distance. If the lifestyle you want involves a four-hour work week rather than working seven days a week for the foreseeable future, something's got to give.

You're assessing the sacrifices involved to achieve your goals and taking responsibility for your choices. For example, one of the things I do today is create software to help Internet marketers manage their e-mail lists, build web pages, do SEO tracking and ranking, and so forth. Because today I have such a big fan base, people approach me all the time with software ideas that could make a lot of money. But I turn down most requests because I'm not ready to make the trade-offs of family and personal time, including vacations. Sacrifices can also include staying fit and getting enough sleep.

Think about the kind of lifestyle you want. Do you want to go into an office or work from home? Do you want the freedom of waking up without an alarm clock? Figure out whether what you have to do to create that life is worth it.

BLOWING AWAY THE PASTOR

Kari and I began defining our goals early on as a couple. When we were in the initial stages of planning our wedding, we agreed to marriage preparation classes at the request of Kari's parents. The classes were held in a little brown-and-white church in a strip mall in Germantown, a village in Wisconsin. The pastor leading the class was a tall guy in his sixties with an air of authority. We were a little intimidated by him.

Because of how young we were, the pastor assumed we didn't know what we were doing. It felt like he thought he had us all figured out. He started drilling us with questions about our future, as if he was determined to change our minds about getting married.

Most of the questions were about whether we were prepared to be on our own. When we started talking about putting 20 percent down on a house and making sure we also had enough money for private mortgage insurance, he was blown away. He didn't realize how much we had drilled down into specifics.

Not many people our age at the time were talking about finances in such detail. The pastor had expected us to be clueless, but we had done our homework. The lesson here: Always do your homework.

FINDING YOUR INNER GPS

Defining your goals also means removing yourself from looking for external validation. Doing so only leads to disappointment. The only thing that will truly help you define your goals is following your inner GPS, and everyone experiences this differently. When you find yours, that's the beginning of trust.

When you rely on what you feel deep down to guide you, what other people think stops mattering. Even though it's only a TV show, *House* is a great way to see this in action; the main character, a quirky rebellious doctor, always follows his gut, even when people think he's crazy. In real life, *Rich Dad Poor Dad* author Robert Kiyosaki faced pushback from friends and family when he decided to become a real estate investor. If he hadn't, millions of people today wouldn't be benefiting from his wisdom.

When we do things for other people's approval, we always end up resenting them anyway, right? What you have is a lose-lose situation. That's what I learned from the struggle with Kari's family over our marriage. We couldn't make decisions based on wanting to make them happy.

If you're making a choice for someone else and it doesn't make you happy, chances are you aren't going to give that choice your all. As a result, your lukewarm efforts will almost certainly disappoint the person from whom you're seeking approval.

HOW TO CHUNK

The best way to begin to achieve your goals is to break them down into smaller, bite-size pieces. I call this chunking. When I have a goal such as building a new software program, before I go to bed I write the goal on my white-board. Then I add five smaller tasks underneath it required for the project. When I wake up the next morning, I know exactly what I need to do that day to move the project further along.

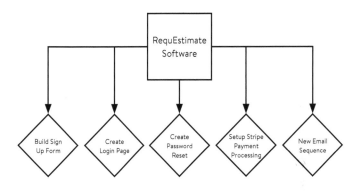

Once a project is done, there's usually a next stage. With a software program, the next step is launching it. I go through the same chunking process with the whiteboard. I write down that I need to create a sales video, a webinar, an e-mail follow-up sequence, and an opt-in page. Underneath each goal, I write down the subtasks required and focus on them step by step in the following days and weeks.

Chunking works because it kills the feeling of being over-whelmed. Chunking creates focus. You can't look at a goal as one big project. You have to look at it as separate components and focus on completing small things each day. One day, the task can be to figure out a password reset; the next, it can be creating the payment processing.

Working this way creates momentum: you look at what you've accomplished each day instead of what you need to do. Working one small step at a time is the antidote to feeling so frustrated with the immensity of a project that you want to quit. The way to go is one chunk at a time.

4

LEVERAGE PAST EXPERIENCES

—

THE FIRST SONG I LEARNED TO PLAY ON guitar was "Nothing Else Matters" by Metallica. The first time I played it, my guitar teacher told me to slow down. I was going far too fast, he said, and every time I hit a wrong string, I was teaching myself a bad habit.

Instead, my teacher had me start off playing superslow: sixty beats per minute on the metronome. After I perfected that, he cranked up the metronome to seventy beats per minute. We kept going until eventually I got up to one hundred and twenty beats per minute...and then finally, I was at full speed, playing the song perfectly and sounding exactly like Metallica (OK, sort of).

As an entrepreneur, when you're reaching for something new, slowing down is often the fastest way to get there.

Once you clearly define what you want to do and successfully reconcile your struggles, the next step is to slow down and leverage past experiences to achieve your goals. I've learned as an entrepreneur that becoming successful is by no means a magical journey. It's not about blind luck or everything falling into place. I realized this after my failed attempts to get a record deal.

In addition, when I first started as an Internet marketer, I reached out to people in the field who were bigger than I was and asked for help and advice. I was hoping their support and connections would anoint me for success. My time would have been better spent working on my own business and learning new skills like copywriting. Musician John Mayer once said of aspiring rock stars, "They're trying to come up with a band name before they even know how to play guitar." I was a little like that.

The best advice I can give you is that you don't need anyone else to make you great. When you do the hard yards and make yourself great, that's what sparks everything. With the power of the Internet, word about you and your work will travel fast. I want to shake you out of any mindset that the power to be and have what you want is dependent on being "discovered."

THE POWER OF MISTAKES

By the time I left nursing school, I had made countless mistakes. I had tried things out, and many of them hadn't worked. I could have given up, but I didn't. The reason is that I chose to look at my mistakes as part of a bigger landscape, one that was about learning and growing, not succeeding or failing.

Warren Buffett, one of the most famous financial minds in the world, once said, "It's good to learn from your mistakes. It's better to learn from other people's mistakes." I live my life by that principle. Growing up, many of my cousins got hooked on drugs and alcohol and ruined their lives. By witnessing their mistakes from an early age, I knew that wasn't the road for me. As I got older, I had no desire to touch anything that might cause me to end up an addict.

When I moved into the working world, I encountered coworkers who talked constantly about how they hated their jobs and careers. One guy at the heating company, Dennis, disliked being an installer so much that he was always trying to go home early or leave a job half-done. He complained all day long about work. I became determined to never end up spending my life getting good at doing the wrong thing.

REEXAMINING FRIENDSHIPS

Around this time, I began to reexamine my friendships. I saw that I had relationships I could leverage to grow and learn from and others that were no longer making a meaningful contribution to my life. For example, I'd known my friend Bobby since elementary school (we first met in the cafeteria after he complimented me on my Sonic the Hedgehog sneakers). He's always been into computers and was learning HTML even before junior high. If Microsoft had ever started a division made up of kid employees, he would have been one of the first hires. As Bobby moved on to high school and college, he got more serious about programming.

As we grew older, I leveraged Bobby's knowledge. I learned about different programming languages: which were designed for website aesthetics and which were better for function. Even though I never became a programmer, just by being around Bobby, I learned much of what I needed to know to eventually create a successful software company myself.

Bobby was also mature and responsible. In my late teens and early twenties, none of my other friends were that way. They were partying most of the time or at home playing *World of Warcraft*; they weren't concerned with finding a career. From the time I started at the heating company,

I'd always been driven to find work that mattered and that paid well. Bobby was the same way.

Eventually, I had to let go of my going-nowhere friends. It was uncomfortable, but I knew that if I didn't do it, they would hold me back. Being around them felt like putting on an old pair of pants or shirt that didn't fit anymore.

Kari and I, as a couple, also experienced losses in friendship. We had once been a constant presence on our local music scene. But as we got more focused on learning how to be successful in Internet marketing, we stopped going to concerts and shows. We spent hours online learning the business. During one period of our lives, we were so driven that we were staying up all night working on growing our company. One of our best friends was Kenny, a member of my band. The three of us were like Harry, Ron, and Hermione from *Harry Potter*. Kenny was like a family member; we exchanged gifts every holiday. But as Kenny got older, he started to go down a different path than we did, one that involved a lot of partying. It was painful when Kari and I realized that the friendship wasn't going to last.

I want to normalize this experience for you. It's not a question of whether your friendships will change but rather how. When friends fall away, it's critical not to feel guilty and believe it's your fault. Life is demanding when you're an entrepreneur, and sacrifices have to be made. But they're worth it.

EVALUATING PREVIOUS JOBS

Another way I leveraged past experiences was to evaluate the work I had done at previous jobs. Being in a band, for example, taught me how to cultivate a fan base. We had created thousands of followers through social media. One of the ways we did that was by going to the Mall of America in Minneapolis, walking around with headphones, and asking people to listen to our music. If they liked it, we'd sell them a four-song CD for $5. We sold a ton.

After a while, I realized that what I was doing wasn't just about music. I was getting great at marketing. Instead of being solely focused on sales, I was learning to nurture and grow a fan base and make people feel like they were part of something. Our music had an outsider vibe that many people, especially creative types, were drawn to. Grassroots marketing like this is common today, but at that time, it was rare. We were one of the first bands to give music away for free online as a way to build an audience.

When I moved on to my Internet business, I took those marketing skills with me. I treated customers as friends and worked to create a sense of community and identity around my products, as I'd done with the band. My business grew quickly because of those skills. Today, I've created a tribe around my work.

I also leveraged what I learned at the heating company to envision what kind of business environment I wanted. I learned that I didn't want a company with huge overhead, numerous employees, and trucks. I didn't want to worry about employee theft or handle the complexities of worker's compensation. I also realized I didn't want to come into an office every day. Two of my top priorities for work were freedom and flexibility.

PLANTING SEEDS

Part of being a successful entrepreneur is constantly trying new things, keeping what works, and abandoning what doesn't. You can't fear failing. You have to follow your interests and your instincts. For a brief period, Kari and I started a T-shirt company. We modeled it after successful apparel companies that sponsored bands and grew their customer base when fans wanted to wear what the musicians were wearing. During another period, we thought about starting a company that sold ads on place mats that were given to restaurant companies for free. We were constantly experimenting.

The beginning of my quest to experiment and find the right road for me started late one winter night when I was roughly eighteen; I was googling around online and came across the Rich Jerk. I clicked on a pop-up ad, and there was a video of a man sitting in a robe, Hugh Hefner style, surrounded by models in a hot tub. In another part of the video, he sat on a toilet using toilet paper made of hundred-dollar bills. He was a wealthy, crazy guy calling people losers and telling them they'd never make anything of their lives.

In fact, the Rich Jerk was the creation of an Internet marketer using reverse psychology to try to both sell his products and help people become successful entrepreneurs. The marketer had hired an actor to create the character. I wasn't curious about how the Rich Jerk was making money or his teaching methods. I wanted to know who the mastermind was behind the bizarre creation. I loved it. But as much as I tried, I couldn't find out who was behind the Rich Jerk.

I bought the course; it was my first introduction to Internet marketing and validated the concept for me. Before that, I hadn't even known the field existed. As a result, I learned about affiliate marking for the first time and made several small commissions promoting a dating website. Then I became distracted by the demands of my band and forgot about the course for several years. I had no idea at that time that the Rich Jerk, a loud-mouthed dude in sunglasses and a leopard-print robe, would play a huge role in my life several years down the road. I'll talk about this in more detail later, in chapter six.

Learning of the Rich Jerk was the first time I had an inkling that maybe I didn't have to work for anyone else. A thought took root: If other people could become entrepreneurs, why not me?

YOU CAN FIGURE ANYTHING OUT

Every past experience can be leveraged for future success. From working at the heating company, I learned that you can figure anything out—especially when you must. As I moved on to new responsibilities, from doing accounts payable and receivable to installing furnaces, I received very little instruction. I was expected to do what needed to be done and not ask questions. Out on a call, if I didn't know how to connect the fresh-air intake vent on a furnace, it was up to me to make it happen and keep my cool during the process.

I learned things by trial and error, and I ultimately learned that when you make mistakes, it's not a big deal; you just fix them. So many people are terrified of making mistakes that they don't try things out. They think they need every single piece of information before taking action. As a result, they become overwhelmed and paralyzed, and they never act. You don't need all the information before jumping in; you can learn along the way.

For example, when Kari and I started out and were scraping by, she began buying clothes at Goodwill and other thrift stores and selling them on eBay. We didn't even know back then that what she was doing was called e-commerce.

Today, Kari runs the e-commerce side of our business, and many of the skills she uses to do so were learned from those first eBay efforts. She learned about copywriting, SEO, and dealing with customers, along with the nuts and bolts of pricing and shipping.

Don't hesitate to dive in like Kari did. As the saying goes, "The worst enemy of a good plan is a perfect plan."

5

BE PREPARED TO STEER OR CHANGE DIRECTION

WHEN I WAS SIXTEEN, I TOOK MY nephew and niece, Ed and Samantha (aka Sam), to see the Canadian rock band Sum 41. They were playing at Summerfest in downtown Milwaukee. I had recently gotten my driver's license and wasn't crazy about dealing with the monster traffic that comes with the eleven-day music festival each year. So I decided to use park and ride. I parked in the designated lot next to the freeway, and a city bus picked us up and took us to the concert.

It was late when the concert let out. The bus was full of rowdy, drunk people. I felt protective of Eddie and Sam, who were only around eight and twelve years old. The bus dropped us off at College Avenue, where I had parked. I looked around for my black Chevy Silverado, but it wasn't there.

I walked around the lot five or six times, frantically looking for my vehicle, but it had vanished. I figured I must have gotten towed, but I was certain I had parked legally. I pulled out my cell phone to call a friend or a family member for a ride, but the phone was dead. As my nephew started to cry, I started to panic.

By this time, it was midnight. I decided the only option—and it wasn't a good one—was to walk to my dad's house several miles away. We had to first walk over a freeway bridge in the inky blackness. As we headed over the bridge, I saw something on the left side of the bridge. I squinted and there it was: another park-and-ride lot. I didn't realize College Avenue had two, and my truck was parked in the other one. The two parking lots were identical, just on different sides of the freeway. Relief flooded my body.

EXPECT CHANGE

When I couldn't find my truck that night, I felt lost. But all I needed to do was look at the situation differently and change my direction. That's what I want you to remember as an entrepreneur. Life is never smooth sailing; stuff happens and we all get derailed. We all panic when that happens. But with flexibility and adaptability, you can ultimately move things to your advantage.

The key is to get comfortable with pivoting and readjusting to changing circumstances. Life moves fast today, probably faster than at any other point in history. The reason why some people are standing still and others are catching waves is that the second group is willing to adapt to change. The people finding happiness and success are those who think on their feet. They're aware that change is unavoidable, and they're ready for it. They *expect* change.

DIAGNOSING PASSION

Most of you reading this book want to pursue your passion, yet there seems to be a disconnect about what it is and how to find it, right?

I recommend writing down not only what you're passionate about but also *why*. Write down the traits, reasons, and skills behind your passion. By discovering the why, you can pinpoint whether you're better suited for one direction over another. For example, when I was wavering on nursing school, I wrote down all the reasons I wanted to be in the profession. I realized that I was passionate about figuring out problems, such as coming up with medical diagnoses. The best nurses are driven by a desire to care for and nurture people. I consider myself a caring person, but I don't have the passion for expressing it through being a nurse.

When you reassess your passions, underlying reasons surface that often point you in a different direction.

It's important to ask yourself, "Is this really what I can see myself doing for the rest of my life?" When I asked myself that question about becoming a nurse, the answer was a resounding no. Same for being on tour for the rest of my days as a musician.

But when I asked myself if I could envision being in Internet marketing for the long haul, the answer was a great big yes.

SURF, EVEN IF YOU'RE AFRAID OF SHARKS

Many people feel stuck when it comes to identifying their passions, as well as their hobbies and interests. One way to become unstuck is to get outside your comfort zone. Cultivate hobbies and interests you've never explored before. Accept invitations from people you might have said no to in the past; go surfing even if you're afraid of sharks. When you get outside your comfort zone, you tap into new parts of yourself and new energies.

You don't have to get outside your comfort zone forever, just long enough to shake things up and until you can identify a new direction.

You've also got to take risks. Sometimes it's a financial risk, such as when I opted out of nursing school after having already paid for most of it. Other times, it's personal, such as moving to a new city by yourself and weathering loneliness. You won't find your way to your purpose through a stroke of luck or by waiting for something to happen to you. You'll only find it by taking a leap of faith.

LOOK AT WHAT PEOPLE DO

One mistake people make in dealing with change and trying to find their passion is to believe they need to reinvent the wheel to find their way. As I mentioned in chapter two, the smarter move is to reverse engineer what someone you admire is doing. Success leaves clues, as motivational speaker Tony Robbins says.

The way to start reverse engineering is to pay attention not to what someone says but to what they do. What are their habits? If you're trying to sell a product that's similar to what a successful person is selling, what does her sales funnel look like? If the person you admire owns a successful bakery similar to one you'd like to own, what does it look like inside? How is the bakery marketed? Are they giving away free samples? Again, look at what they *do*.

It's easy to find content online about a person or company you want to emulate. Read everything you can about them. Find out what they're doing differently than their competitors. Analyze their website and the process you went through when they brought you on board as a customer. I encourage you to be bold and interview people not only about what made them successful but also about their mistakes.

In addition, observe how they introduce products. Apple, for example, creates an incredible sense of drama around their product launches. As a result, countless people line up the night before a new iPhone is launched.

Going back to my days as a musician, at a certain point, I saw that the music industry was tanking. It was freaking out about the rise of technology and how no one was buying CDs anymore. I began to worry less about selling CDs and more about cultivating a fan base and marketing. The goal was to build a strong brand. I decided to start giving our band's music away like the forward-thinking bigger fish were doing. We ended up winning a major award as a local band among stiff competition that included much bigger groups. I reverse engineered, I adapted, and I pivoted.

WHAT YOU GET FROM LETTING GO

Pivoting requires sacrifice. There's no way around it. In order to go to nursing school, I had to sell my truck. When my mom lost her house, we had to move in with my brother. When I decided to leave nursing school, I had to sacrifice my dream of a secure job with a steady paycheck and health insurance.

But it's important to keep holding the big picture. These types of sacrifices are almost always temporary losses in service to a bigger dream.

Sacrifices aren't always about material things. After Kari and I got married, we were out of touch with her parents and a large part of her extended family for close to a year. We were intently focused on our business, but underneath that were painful feelings about our marriage not having their support.

I can see now that the lack of contact pushed us into finding our own way as adults. Today, as I said, our relationship is strong and healthy. We learned, and I hope you do, too, that by letting go, you always gain something in the long run.

6

IT'S NOT ALL IN THE TIMING

—

I N THE AGE OF THE INTERNET, MANY PEOPLE
are finding themselves in a weird relationship with
time. Your past, for example, is your present when
you see what your old high school friends are doing
on Facebook every day. Author Douglas Rushkoff wrote
about this phenomenon in his 2013 book *Present Shock*.
Other people today, from thought leaders to physicists,
often talk about time through the lens of quantum physics:
time's not linear, they say, but everything's happening simultaneously.

But one view of time that hasn't changed for most of us
is the concept that we need to wait for the right time to
be successful—that it all comes down to getting a big
break. But waiting for the right time has nothing to do
with achieving success.

There's a difference between timing and focus. Forget about "my time will come." Put in the hard work and it will pay off. It's the difference between waiting to win the lottery and saving a few thousand dollars a year and watching the money compound. Time can work in your favor, but only if you let it.

I'm not saying that you don't need other people to help you along the way. I don't discount luck as a factor in success. But as the saying goes, luck is when preparation meets opportunity. If you've invested your time and energy well, people will recognize that you're worth investing in. In my opinion, your only relationship with time should involve you putting in the time to meet your goals.

When you do that, it's always the right time.

A BLAST FROM THE PAST

One night when we were still living at my brother's place, I was sitting in front of my computer after finishing my homework for nursing school. It was around eleven o'clock. I was feeling bleak; in the two years since I had started school, wages for nurses had dropped from about $65,000 or $75,000 a year to $35,000 or $40,000. A glut of nursing school graduates was flooding the field.

By now, I was approximately $35,000 in debt with student loans. It was nerve-racking. I didn't want to graduate and feel like I'd wasted a huge amount of time and money. In addition, when Kari and I had moved in together, she had helped me pay off a big chunk of previous debt so we could start our lives on the right track. She had saved up that money through her own hard work. I didn't want to let her down through my own bad choices. I wanted to make her proud.

I looked around the room where we were living. All our stuff was jam-packed into the ex-garage. We were sleeping on a worn futon. Our cat, Ling-Ling, and our Yorkie, Tinkerbell, were on top of us every day. No bathroom.

As I sat in front of my computer at a cheap rolling desk, I knew I had to do something to move us forward. Now.

A thought popped into my head: I wonder what the Rich Jerk is up to? If you remember, he was the Internet character I mentioned in chapter four. The Rich Jerk was the creation of a mysterious Internet marketer. The obnoxious character used reverse psychology to help people become successful entrepreneurs.

I googled around and eventually came across a blog for Kelly Felix. Finally, I had discovered the mastermind behind the Rich Jerk. In one blog post, Felix described how the wealth he had acquired by creating the Rich Jerk had ended up ruining his life. Friends had taken advantage of him. He had gotten sucked into buying cars and houses and other stuff he didn't need. A bad divorce had impacted him personally and professionally.

Felix went on to write that he had taken a year or two off and had just created a new product called Bring The Fresh. Felix said he had recently rebuilt his entire business around SEO, and Bring The Fresh was a course that taught people everything he had learned.

I had a gut instinct to buy Bring The Fresh. It was a lot of money for me at the time, roughly $67 a month for six or seven months. But intuition told me to take the risk. I felt empowered by my determination to change our lives and the possibility that Bring The Fresh would help.

Through Bring The Fresh, I learned the mechanics of building a website without needing programming skills, via WordPress. I learned how to optimize the site for key words, researching which were worth using and ranking, and where to place them on the site. I also learned how to buy domain names and use backlinking.

At that time in nursing school, I was taking an anatomy

and physiology course. Through what I learned from Bring The Fresh, I created a website to help students complete their homework assignments, much of which involved memorizing muscles and bones. I monetized the site with an affiliate marketing product: flash cards that helped students with memorization.

Bring The Fresh made a big impact on my life. While still in school, by using what I had learned in the course, I started to bring in more income. I hadn't waited for something to happen; I had made it happen. I'll talk more about Bring The Fresh and what I learned in more detail in the next chapter.

When I started to bring in more money through SEO and affiliate marketing, Kari and I decided to move out of my brother's place. The move was a turning point. I found a guy on Craigslist who was subletting his apartment for the next six months for $900 a month. The place was located in Sussex, a nice community where my wife had grown up. It had two bedrooms with a decent-sized living room and a little dining room attached to the kitchen. It was located on the first floor with a patio, so we could easily let the dog out. The neighborhood had a community center and a park nearby.

Moving out was a risk, but I calculated that if SEO sales

kept going the way they were, our income would climb. I kept following my intuition. Two months after we moved into the new place, the business was scaling fast, and that's when I made the leap to leave both nursing school and my job. I decided to focus solely on growing the business, and Kari joined me.

Kari took over selling backlinks to other people, and I took on SEO clients. More and more clients came on; by the end of year one, we were on track to make six figures annually.

When our lease was up, we found a new, bigger apartment we liked even better. Halfway through that second lease, we decided we wanted to buy a house. The bank wouldn't approve us for a loan because we needed two years of self-employment history. On the two-year mark, we got approved in a flash and bought a beautiful, seventeen-hundred-square-foot house in West Bend, my brother's neighborhood. A year later, we moved again, this time to a five-thousand-square-foot house in West Bend, where we live today. The house sits on a couple of acres and has seven bedrooms and a movie theater room.

We no longer sleep on a futon but a Tempur-Pedic mattress. By using our time to focus on our business, we grew exponentially.

A FAMILY COMES TOGETHER

In the middle of building our business, a triggering event occurred. Kari's paternal grandmother, who was already undergoing cancer treatment, had a stroke. Seeing Kari's parents at the hospital was awkward at first, but the situation forced all of us to communicate again.

After the stroke, Grandma Jackie lost her ability to talk. She hung on for a while longer, going first to rehab and then a nursing home, where she eventually passed away. It was a monumental loss because we had grown extremely close to her and that side of the family. They had supported us emotionally when it felt like other branches of the family weren't behind our relationship.

No one saw the death coming. Grandma Jackie was energetic and full of life, slender with long blond hair. She used to love cutting the grass and sitting out in the backyard with her radio, listening to her beloved Milwaukee Brewers play baseball. Everyone joked that even in her seventies, she routinely turned men's heads at the grocery store and everywhere she went.

As the family grieved, the old hurts about our relationship and the wedding didn't seem as important anymore. In the meantime, our business was growing more and more successful, and Kari's parents started to see that their fears about our ability to support ourselves were unfounded.

While my dad had always been encouraging of our new business, my mom had, like Kari's parents, expressed fears and concerns about it working out. Around this time, she, too, came to see that we knew what we were doing and where we were going. It was amazing to receive the love and respect Kari and I had both wanted from our families. But at the same time, we had both changed so much that we didn't need outside validation from anyone, even the people closest to us.

7

SMALL WINS ADD UP

IT WAS OCTOBER AND GETTING COLDER OUT-side. Inside my brother's clubhouse, I could feel the turn in the weather. I sat in front of my laptop hitting the refresh button every few minutes. I hit refresh one more time, and there it was. I yelled to Kari that $20 had just landed in my account on ClickBank, an affiliate marketing site. It was one of the most exciting things that had ever happened to me. The $20, a commission on my first sale, was validation that Internet marketing was going to change our future.

Success doesn't happen in one big swoop; it's about small wins that add up. That $20 was the first of many small wins that snowballed and created what I have today: personal and financial freedom.

The idea that created the win came to me in nursing school

while I was doing my anatomy homework between classes. I ran across a question I couldn't answer. It was something like:

Q. What is the name for the lower part of the sternum?

When I googled around, a bunch of question-and-answer sites like Yahoo Answers popped up. I found the answer on one:

A. The xiphoid process.

As I clicked around the different question-and-answer sites, I saw that hardly anyone was answering people's homework questions. I got the idea of answering questions, linking back to a question-and-answer site of my own specializing in anatomy and physiology, and monetizing the site by selling a third-party product: flash cards for studying.

That's what I did. When I answered questions, I'd cite my own website as the source in order to drive traffic there. I'd also make up questions and answers for other sites and, again, backlink to mine. Loads of traffic started arriving on my site.

To many people, $20 might not seem like much. But on

that October night, the first commission from the flash cards (created by an entrepreneurial doctor) was proof of concept. It said to me that we were going places.

From there, things moved quickly. I branched out to other affiliate marketing opportunities, such as linking to sites that provided information on student loans. I learned how to set up Google AdSense and get paid every time someone clicked on an affiliate's banner. Commissions quickly began to compound.

At school, instead of studying between classes I was refreshing my ClickBank account every few minutes and watching the numbers go higher and higher. Within a very short time, I realized I could pursue the work full time. I quit nursing school and ran with it.

SNOWBALLING INTO A NEW ARENA

I took my early success in Internet marketing and put my own creative twist on it: helping local businesses gain more clients through SEO. I was inspired to do it from thinking back to my days at the heating company. I remembered how much solicitation we received from salespeople wanting us to hire them to increase our customer base. But none of their ideas revolved around ranking us on Google. They offered instead features such as sending out a thousand flyers to potential customers.

Even though I was no longer working there, I decided to use the heating company as my guinea pig. Google Maps (then called Google Places) had a feature called a seven-pack. It was a box of seven listings that popped up in response to a search in your city, but only three listings were visible without clicking through.

I used SEO to get the heating company ranked in the top three listings for furnace repair, and calls began pouring in. New clients followed.

My SEO business grew quickly. I used the same technique with my clients as I did when I was looking for my dream house. I asked them how many new clients they needed on a weekly basis to achieve their financial goals.

Small business owners didn't necessarily care about being on the first page of Google; they didn't know what backlinking, optimization, and key word research meant. But when I asked them, "Do you want your phone to ring?" I almost always gained a new client. I spoke their language. As the saying goes, features tell and benefits sell.

One of my first clients was a dentist, Dr. P. I went to her

to have a cavity filled shortly after we moved to Sussex. In the dentist's chair, I mentioned to Dr. P. how it had taken me a few Google pages to find her and shared what I was doing with SEO. She was passionate about educating people on the importance of oral health and listened hard. She had a marketing person helping with her website and branding but hadn't yet pursued SEO. Dr. P. soon hired me. Our game plan was based on research she had done that found that potential clients don't want to travel more than fifteen minutes for a dental appointment. I designed an SEO campaign to bring in customers within a fifteen-mile radius. Within thirty days, Dr. P. was gaining fifteen new clients a month.

Another client was a DJ, Finn, referred to me by my former music producer. Finn was a smart, decent, edgy guy getting his MBA in finance. He planned to DJ on the side to help pay for it. He was starting from scratch. I created a digital presence for him, including a website and logo. I also got him ranked high in the wedding DJ category in three different Wisconsin areas: Milwaukee, Brookfield, and New Berlin. Finn's business blew up. He was getting thirty calls a month from people wanting to hire him. Finn's worries about how he was going to pay off his student loans started to disappear.

HOW I SCALED MY BUSINESS

After I'd successfully helped about six small business clients, I decided to create a training program. At that time, as far as I could tell, no presence yet existed on the web for helping local business owners use SEO.

I stumbled across Warrior Forum, an Internet marketing community and marketplace. I created a course to sell on the forum of roughly thirty videos outlining what I had done for clients like Dr. P. and Finn. It was called Busy Business Bonanza. Kari and I shot it on a little Kodak camera that I had bought for $150. Production was bare bones: I set the camera up on tripod in the living room of our Sussex apartment and just stood against a white wall during filming.

I was nervous about releasing the course; sleepless nights dogged me. I was worried about ruining my reputation if people thought it was crap. Finally, I summoned up the nerve and posted information about the course in the classified section of Warrior Forum. I asked if anyone would be willing to review it for me; in exchange, I would provide the course for free. I didn't have name recognition and needed to build a presence. Five people took me up on my offer and wrote great reviews.

I moved forward and launched the $27 course in the Special Offers section of the forum. My sales page was awful because I didn't know anything about copywriting. But I did have the five reviews and a decent three-minute video that showed how I was generating leads for clients.

Interest came in right away. People started asking questions and a handful of sales followed. Soon, I heard from bigger marketers who told me they had purchased the course and liked it. They offered suggestions on how to improve the sales copy. The marketers wanted to recommend the course to their own customers, but because my page was so rough, they weren't comfortable making a recommendation until I upped my game.

I took their advice. Marketers began promoting the course on their e-mail lists, and sales started flooding in by the hundreds. In forty-five days, I had sold roughly two thousand copies, making over $50,000.

All of a sudden, I had established myself as an expert in local marketing. The homegrown vibe of the course had worked to my advantage. Customers posted that they liked how down-to-earth I came across and that they appreciated that I was using examples from real clients and real sites.

ONE SUCCESS LED TO ANOTHER

Busy Business Bonanza was a game changer for me. From its popularity, I eventually grew my e-mail list and audience to more than twenty-five thousand people.

I branched out into creating different software tools like RequEstimate, which helps sell sales leads generated through Google rankings. Another tool, Maps Prospector, locates all the business owners via Google Maps who haven't verified their listing. It provides contact information for Internet marketers who want to approach them about being an SEO client.

In addition, Kari and I moved into what's called retail arbitrage; we learned the ins and outs from a woman named Joy who had bought Busy Business Bonanza. Retail arbitrage involves buying items from local stores—from jewelry to toys—and reselling them on Amazon at a higher price. But we discovered it was hard to tell how fast any given item would sell. I developed a mobile app called Rank Informer to help people make better purchasing decisions: Rank Informer lets you know how quickly the item will sell based on its rank compared to competing products on Amazon's best seller lists.

A pattern developed: I'd create a marketing tool that I needed for myself and then leverage it by selling it to other people. What separated me from other Internet marketers is that from the start, I treated my customers like a band treats fans. I put out a huge amount of free training materials via YouTube videos and worked to make people feel like they were part of a tribe. Meanwhile, my identity and how I looked at life started to shift as a result of all the feedback about how I was changing people's lives. I began to focus more on serving and helping people in the best way possible than on how much money I was earning.

In four years, I went from a struggling student on the wrong career track, with thousands of dollars of debt, to a top Internet marketer with a mission. From teaching SEO to building software to working in e-commerce, it all started with that first $20 commission from a pack of flash cards. My best advice to you: Don't get bogged down in the big picture of how things will unfold. Pick a place to start and take one step forward...and then another. It's all about small wins.

8

YOUR BIG BREAK (IS YOU)

—

WE HAD JUST PURCHASED OUR FIRST home and expenses were piling up. We were putting a new hardwood floor in the dining room and painting nearly the entire house, starting with a dark chocolate brown in the living room and pale green for my office. In addition, we had bought a top-of-the-line, front-loading washer and dryer. They were big and stainless steel; the pedestals alone cost more than $200 each. For the first time, we had property taxes due—about $3,500.

Even though my business was taking off, thanks to selling the training courses on how I'd started my digital marketing agency, we were spending so much on stuff that I was starting to dip into the money I'd set aside for property taxes.

I kept thinking that all I needed to do was connect with one major Internet marketer—a celebrity in the field—and things would blow up. I would never have to worry about bills again. I set my sights on a marketer I'll call Ron, whom I'd seen on a television infomercial telling his story. When Ron was in college, his parents had lost everything in the stock market. Ron had been forced to drop out of business school. He said he decided to learn everything he could about Internet marketing and, in a very short time, was generating tens of thousands of dollars. In the infomercial, Ron pitched the book he had written that revealed how he did it. He was smooth talking, compelling, and well known, and his audience numbered in the hundreds of thousands.

Scott was a digital Internet marketer and a business partner of Ron's. Scott and I were acquaintances and Facebook friends; after I had given him free access to one of my courses, we stayed in touch. I threw out an idea to Scott about the three of us creating a course together to teach local marketing through SEO.

Scott thought it was a fantastic idea; he broached it with Ron, who agreed and promised to launch it. We dived in. Ron hired a high-end copywriter for $3,000. He had me doing voice-overs and on-camera work for weeks. Putting everything together was hard work and extremely time-consuming, but I knew it would be worth it in the long run.

Scott thought we could easily make at least $200,000 with the soft launch alone and in only a couple of weeks. My house had cost $200,000, and I was over-the-top excited thinking about how I could pay it off from the course within the first six months.

The time came to launch the course and...nothing happened. Ron sat on it, refusing to release it. He didn't respond to either Scott's or my requests to find out what was going on. It was his responsibility to pay the copywriter, but he never did that either. The copywriter was understandably pissed and came after Scott and me for the money.

The course was never released and I never found out why. Scott and Ron ended up parting ways. Scott kept telling me he'd like to work together on different ventures. He would spin these incredible scenarios about what we could accomplish, but he never followed through on a single thing. I can't begin to describe how disappointed and disillusioned I felt from dealing with both of them. I fell into a funk about the whole experience.

I soon discovered that Ron wasn't making money off his infomercial; he was misleading people via a dishonest sales tactic. People would call in to buy his book, and Ron would sell the leads to what's called a boiler room—a third-party call center—for $80 each. Leads would then be contacted and pushed to buy coaching sessions with Ron and his team. The subscribers never got coached by Ron or another pro but rather by someone sitting in the boiler room reading off a script for $10 an hour.

The failure with Ron had been a blessing in disguise. I didn't want to be associated with anyone who had so little integrity. I felt a little like Dorothy in *The Wizard of Oz* when Toto accidentally unmasks the Wizard as a fraud, an ordinary guy from Omaha.

One April night not long after the whole Ron mess, I finally realized that Ron wasn't my big break. Nobody would be. I was my big break.

I decided to stop thinking someone else was going to change my life and focus instead on creating a game plan to get to Ron's level on my own. I thought about what my skill set was. I knew I was good on video. I decided to grow my YouTube channel as much as possible.

When I decided it was up to me to create my own destiny, everything clicked.

YOU ARE THE ANSWER

If you take away only one thing from this book, I want it to be this: Your big break is you. It has nothing to do with a specific person or a life-altering event. It's not about blind luck or timing. It's about your hard work. If you want to lose weight, you will get nowhere buying a treadmill and then sticking it in your basement to gather dust. You will not lose weight standing still or through treadmill osmosis. You have to take the initiative and start moving.

I know how challenging it is to change the way you may have been thinking your whole life. As an example: for centuries, people thought the world was flat, right? Then when hard evidence came that the world was round, everyone had to shift their thinking to grasp the new reality. I'm asking you to completely shift your ideas about what it takes to become successful. When you do that, then you can make new choices about how to navigate life.

By trusting yourself, digging deep to generate your own confidence and drive, and ignoring the naysayers, you will chart a new course. I know that if I can do it, so can you. I entered an industry I knew nothing about and created an entirely new reality for myself.

As I mentioned, one of the ways I did that was by reverse engineering what people I admired were doing. To build a community for my videos, for example, I borrowed techniques from YouTube celebrity gamers. I held live streams in which I showed exactly how to build out websites, including the SEO. I let people comment and ask questions throughout the stream. I was transparent about my strategy, like well-known *World of Warcraft* gamers are about how they defeat a raid.

Another thing I did was give away free software, like bands were doing with their music. One of my inspirations at the time was Christofer Drew of Never Shout Never. He built such a huge fan base on his own that he was able to create his own record label.

As I mentioned in the last chapter, I created an app, Maps Prospector, that found unverified Google Maps listings, generating leads for Internet marketers. I created a simple Facebook ad campaign to give away the app for a limited time. Through that one campaign, I built an e-mail list of five thousand people who remain on my e-mail list today. I've sold them many other different products since that first free offer.

Through focusing on mining my talents and creating great content, my business grew exponentially. I leveraged my time differently than before, and it paid off.

If you're stuck in an old mindset about waiting for success to happen to you, you'll waste time chasing the wrong things. The opportunity to make creative decisions like reverse engineering other people's success will fall by the wayside. You'll never really get that your big break is you.

It's critical to redefine your goals. Ask yourself: "Is how I'm spending my time furthering those goals? Or am I wasting time on unproductive ideas and tasks?" Focus every single day on what you can do to continually grow into the life you want to be living. When I was waiting on someone like Ron to make me a success, a sense of randomness filled my days. I was gambling and hoping for a payoff. Focus fills my days now.

You have to think for yourself. Maybe it is ingrained in your head, as it was in mine, that you have to go to college. But thousands of people are graduating from college today with unbelievable debt and few job prospects. Both my family and Kari's thought we'd made a mistake by passing up college...until we bought our second house on a lake. They came over the day we closed and saw the two-and-a-half acres of woods the house sits on, the granite countertops in the kitchen, and the whirlpool tub in the master bedroom, among other things. It was five thousand beautiful square feet of proof that we had known what path was best for us.

"Never say you can't do something," my brother Ed advised me years ago. "You can always figure out how to do it."

That's the mindset I have today. I moved from a life of fear-based thinking to one where I know I can always figure out how to make something work and lead the life I want. My success wasn't random but deliberate, shaped by the six insights I came to through all my ups and downs. The insights are, again:

- **Reframe your struggles.**
- **Define who you want to be.**
- **Leverage past experiences.**
- **Be prepared to steer or change course.**
- **It's not all in the timing.**
- **Small wins add up.**

I've coached countless clients using the six insights. Jeff came to me wanting to get better at SEO. He thought his so-so grasp of it was the only reason his performance as an Internet marketer had been mediocre so far. I reframed his struggle and convinced him that instead of focusing on learning SEO, he needed to focus on learning how to sell. I coached him to find unverified listings through Maps Prospector and offer to verify listings for free for potential clients. By building goodwill and trust up front, he could then ask if they wanted to hire him to increase their rankings.

Jeff immediately went out and landed a mortgage company client for $1,500 per month. He improved his SEO skills along the way through that first small win. Today, he's making more than $20,000 in recurring income each month from SEO clients.

Lamont had been working as a mortgage officer but wanted to spend more time with his family. Nine months after taking my courses and studying my training materials, he was able to quit his job. Today, he runs an Internet marketing company with his son, who will now be able to pay for college because of their financial success.

John wanted to work as an Internet marketer but was afraid to do so because of Google's constant changes and updates; he worried that he couldn't keep up. I convinced him that the complexity was a good thing because it gave his clients a reason to keep working with him. While everyone else was panicking, he would be adapting and evolving, I explained. John was able to push through his fear and now works full time for himself.

NOTHING IS STATIC

Jeff, Lamont, and John went through obstacles and self-doubt, but they were still able to change their lives. So can you. Nothing is static. Where you are today doesn't have to define tomorrow.

If you've read this far, you can tell how passionate I am about helping people find the freedom I've found in work and in life. That's why I'm offering readers of this book special trainings and resources at no cost to give you a leg up. Go to pauljames.com/bigbreak to find them.

The six insights make up your golden ticket. The difference is, unlike Charlie in *Charlie and the Chocolate Factory*, you don't have to wait for a stroke of luck to find the ticket wrapped in a chocolate bar. Always remember: You are your own golden ticket.

ACKNOWLEDGMENTS

This book would not have been possible without the support of my wife, Kari. She has always been behind me 100 percent, from supporting me as a musician to helping to pay off my debt when we started our lives together. I'm grateful to have a life partner who is also such an amazing and dedicated business partner.

I also want to thank both our families and extended families. Thanks to everyone on my editorial team, including Jeremy Brown, Katherine Songster, and Leslie Guttman.

Finally, my appreciation to you, the reader, for buying this book and to my tribe of clients and customers. Thank you to everyone who has purchased a product from me, read my e-mails, and watched my videos. Nothing would be possible without you.

ABOUT THE AUTHOR

PAUL JAMES is a widely respected leader in the country's new generation of Internet marketers with a passion for pushing the boundaries of what's possible. A former professional musician, he was an early pioneer in the use of social media as a means of building a thriving fan community. He leveraged his experiences in SEO into a successful online enterprise that enabled local business owners to substantially expand their clientele. Paul currently offers online training courses that have helped countless subscribers find flexible work and financial freedom. He lives in Wisconsin with his wife and business partner, Kari.